JACK NICKLAUS

PHOTO CREDITS
Bruce Curtis: pp. 7, 17, 21, 29, and cover
Carl Skalak, Jr.: pp. 5, 9, 11, 13, 15, 19, 23, 25, 27, 31

Published by Creative Educational Society, Inc.,
123 South Broad Street, Mankato, Minnesota 56001
Library of Congress Cataloging in Publication Data

Taylor, Paula.
Golf's great winner, Jack Nicklaus.
SUMMARY: Concentrates on the famous golfer's style and
his competitiveness with Arnold Palmer.
1. Nicklaus, Jack—Juvenile literature. 2. Golfers
—United States—Biography—Juvenile literature.
[1. Nicklaus, Jack. 2. Golfers] I. Title.
GV964.N5T39   796.352'092'4 [92]   76-45375
ISBN 0-87191-591-X

GOLF'S GREAT WINNER JACK NICKLAUS

BY PAULA TAYLOR

CREATIVE EDUCATION/CHILDRENS PRESS

4

Competition is exciting to Jack Nicklaus. He likes the challenge of playing courses which leave many of his opponents caught in sand traps or stranded in the rough. Difficult shots do not bother him. Playing against the world's top golfers merely sharpens his desire. If a match turns out to be close and he has to come from behind to win — so much the better.

6

Jack Nicklaus won his first major tournament — the National Amateur — in 1959 when he was only 19. Since then he has gone on to win 16 major golf championships — more than any other player. Nicklaus has also designed golf courses and written books about golf. But he still doesn't feel he knows all there is to know about the game.

"You never really master golf," he says. "More often than not, the game masters you."

Jack's modesty may be the key to his success. He doesn't get overconfident. He tries not to think about winning or compare scores with his opponents. Instead, he maps out his strategy hole by hole, shot by shot.

Once a shot is played, Nicklaus has a remarkable ability to dismiss it from his mind. He doesn't brood about landing in a sand trap or let a bad putt ruin his game.

10

"The thing about golf is that it's so mental," says Nicklaus. "It's not a game of reaction; it's a game of thought and correction."

A tennis player has only a few seconds to think about the next shot. A golfer often has five or ten minutes. That's too long for most people. They get distracted. Nicklaus doesn't. He keeps all his attention fixed on the ball.

12

Before a tournament Nicklaus paces out the course, taking note of odd trees, boulders and other landmarks. No matter where his ball lands, he is able to calculate exactly how many yards it is from the pin.

But distance isn't all Jack considers. He also looks at the ball's position. He estimates the wind speed and direction. He decides how fast the ball is likely to run when it hits the green.

He even considers how he feels — he may use a slightly shorter club to compensate for the extra distance he gets "when the adrenalin is flowing."

14

It takes Jack a while to think over all these factors. Early in his career he was often criticized for playing too slowly. Sometimes he was even penalized. So he tried to speed up his play.

But he still insists, "It didn't seem long to me — just long enough to think it out and hit the ball."

16

Jack's ability to shut out distractions helps him when he plays in important tournaments. Then thousands of people follow the players around the course.

Now the galleries hush expectantly when Jack gets ready to shoot. But in 1962, the year Nicklaus broke into professional golf, the fans weren't so polite. They wanted to see Arnie Palmer, not Jack Nicklaus. Wearing buttons labeled "Arnie's Army," they not only cheered their hero but heckled Nicklaus, the 22-year-old newcomer who threatened to upstage him.

18

The hecklers would crouch behind bunkers, holding up signs saying, "Hit It Here, Jack." They cheered his misses and booed his good shots. Once someone even threw a beer can. A reporter covering one tournament remarked that he thought he was at a wrestling match.

But, as usual, Nicklaus was concentrating on his game, rather than on the gallery. "What boos?" he asked afterwards in surprise.

20

Jack didn't let the antics of "Arnie's Army" affect his game. But the fans' rejection hurt, just the same. For years he didn't mention the problem, even to his wife, Barbara. But he thought about it a lot.

Jack realized he could never become another Palmer. Arnie was dashingly handsome. He looked and dressed like a movie star. Jack was overweight. He never thought about his clothes. His pants were always wrinkled and his shirts wouldn't stay tucked in. The floppy hats he wore looked as though they'd been sat on.

Arnie laughed and joked with the crowd as he played. Jack stared at his ball and looked grim.

Arnie would always gamble on an impossible shot. Jack played it safe.

22

Jack knew better than to try to change his personality or the way he played. He just gritted his teeth and shot the best golf he knew how.

In 1962 Jack defeated Arnie Palmer in the U.S. Open. A year later he won both the Masters and the PGA tournaments. Gradually golf fans began to appreciate the disciplined, methodical way Nicklaus played the game.

24

People who got to know Jack found that he wasn't really as cold as he seemed. He made a point of chatting with caddies and scorekeepers, as well as with players and reporters. He always remembered everyone's name and seemed genuinely interested in the people he met.

Jack didn't want to be treated like a celebrity. As one friend remarked, "He's the kind of person you feel you could entertain as easily in your kitchen as in your living room."

26

A few years ago Jack decided he was getting tired too easily. So he went on a diet and lost 20 pounds. Now he's no longer tagged with names referring to his weight. Instead, sportswriters call him the "Golden Bear."

When Jack is playing well, everything feels right. He knows his hands are perfectly aligned on the club. He pivots easily and smoothly as he swings.

Sometimes he loses this feeling. Jack is a remarkably consistent player. But even champions have off-days.

In 1970 Jack had a bad slump. In the U.S. Open that year he tied for 51st place. But he was able to think through what went wrong and correct it. Twenty days later he won the British Open.

30

Jack Nicklaus has been called the greatest golfer of all time. But he himself waves aside such a suggestion.

"It's my objective, of course," he says. "But you have to wait until a man's career is over before you can properly judge him.

"In golf you're always breaking a barrier. When you bust it you set yourself a little higher barrier and try to break that one."

BILLIE JEAN KING
O. J. SIMPSON
EVEL KNIEVEL
HANK AARON
JOE NAMATH
OLGA KORBUT
FRAN TARKENTON
MUHAMMAD ALI
CHRIS EVERT
FRANCO HARRIS
BOBBY ORR
KAREEM ABDUL JABBAR
JACK NICKLAUS
JOHNNY BENCH
JIMMY CONNORS
A. J. FOYT

THE ALLSTARS